Crossing the Lake

by Anna Terrence

illustrated by Margie Moore

Bessy plopped down on the shore.
"We've got to think hard,"
she said to her puppy.

"We need to cross this lake.
Our campsite is on that side,"
said Bessy.
"How can we cross?"asked Puppy.

"I do not like wet lashes or fur,"
said Bessy.
"And I cannot swim," said Puppy
with a cry. "I will sink if I try."

Then Frog dashes up and faces them.
"This is what I'm planning,"
said Frog. "We'll cross together."

"First, sit on this plank," he said.
"It's not going to sink.
Then I will take this ring."

"I will use this short rope to tug.
I will not dunk you as we cross,"
said Frog.
"That is not funny," said Bessy.

Frog tugged and tugged.
Bessy and Puppy hugged him.
"Thank you, our new best friend
for helping us."